RIVER ROAD

Also by Richard Foerster

—⁓—

Transfigured Nights (1990, chapbook)
Sudden Harbor (1992)
The Hours (1993, chapbook)
Patterns of Descent (1993)
Trillium (1998)
Double Going (2002)
The Burning of Troy (2006)
Penetralia (2011)

River Road

POEMS BY

Richard Foerster

Texas Review Press
Huntsville, Texas

FIRST EDITION, 2015

Requests for permission to reproduce material from this work should be sent to:

Permissions
Texas Review Press
English Department
Sam Houston State University
Huntsville, TX 77341-2146

—∿—

Library of Congress Cataloging-in-Publication Data

Foerster, Richard, 1949- author.
  [Poems. Selections]
  River road / Richard Foerster. -- Edition: first.
      pages cm
  ISBN 978-1-68003-053-2 (pbk. : alk. paper)
  1. Grief--Poetry. 2. Love poetry. 3. Life change events--
Poetry. I. Title.
  PS3556.O23A6 2015
  811'.54--dc23

                                        2015018369

for Douglas Taylor

Contents

—∾— I —∾—

—ᛝ— II —ᛝ—

I

. . . the artist pursues clarity in open confusion.
—Thomas Harrison,
1910: The Emancipation of Dissonance

River Road

Let's take the scenic route, he'd sometimes say
on our drives back to my house from Ogunquit
before he'd leave for home. Spur-of-the-moment,
or so it seemed, his impulses forced me to brake hard
and swerve well short of my usual turn on Rte. IA.

Instantly, the mortised angles of our days
would loosen as I shifted to take the curves
past the corner baker's shop. The road
would open then like a mother's oven door and spill
a brief aroma apple-warm across the asphalt.

One time at the bend where the Baptist church
perches on its knoll, he asked, as if insisting,
Wouldn't you love to live on this road?
The bell tower's lead-white caught the sun
and cast a blinding glare upon us.

At the opposite curb, the old colonial
we admired, with its weathered shakes,
squatted like a hen half-hidden in shadows
among bee-balm and a blare of orange lilies.
Yes, I admitted, past the graveyard and the bridge

where the estuary begins to broaden
toward a glimpse of lighthouse and the sea.
The blacktop shimmered that day before us,
itself a flow of water ending at the shore.
We'll build a home here when I'm free.

SUMMER SOLSTICE

Not just, as always, that craving
for light and yet more light,
but the climb, and from that hill
a vista, which by gazing into
we hoped to lose ourselves, poured
out among the fresh-mown fields
and copses pierced here and there
by a steeple's brushstroke,
whitest cadmium, set like a blaze
amid the evening's long divertimento
and feathered edge, the air itself
a Delft-blue powder crazed
with lingering swallows.
                              No words
passed between us, and neither
pressed the other's hand to stay
or go from where we stood
watching mists begin to rise
above the pulsing gold-green
fields, as if from hidden fires,
and yet we turned, as one, back
toward the grassy path that parted
again like a shallow sea before us,
and walked while the near-dark
gathered overhead and its unstoppable
arc spilled like a globe of sand.

MALE NUDE, KNEELING, FROM THE BACK

If I begin at the forelock,
wisp of brow, the swept-up
lash and forget the focus
of his gaze for now,
that roomless room
where the hushed toil
of brush and blade
must have scraped
at his ear over a course
of days, I see how
the shoulder's craquelure
brims yet with blue
subterranean veins,
how the muted
palette delves like a
scalpel to mine each sinew
and curve and render
into light this solid weight,

and I hold him here,
so passively naked,
muscled with repose
and it brings a sadness
each time to think
the broad sloped fields
of his back, the ridge
and canyon, knoll
at his thigh, the dab
of nipple, the callused
sole and tangled knot
that anchors him
in place, the dark furrow
I can't help but trace

toward whatever power
must remain hidden
from view—to think
all he is, and was, is dust.

ABSENCES

. . . as in the way negative space informs
a canvas, forces line and pigment toward

solider realities, beyond illusion—like oxygen,
taken for granted except when it is not there;

. . . as in this photo from '49 after my sister's
courthouse wedding, the name of the restaurant

unknown and thus made relevant to the whole:
the table in less than formal disarray, the festivity

over, and left for a waiter nowhere to be seen;
. . . or in the way the linen's curtained folds confront

the lens to imply a stage set for a different drama,
the act already in progress, or nearly ended—

who can tell? The small party is posed behind
with faint smiles: the raven-haired wife, slim

at eighteen; the groom, swarthed even then
with shadows, his beard ever at 5 p.m. The childless

aunt who loved well, but never married, perches beside
our blond-tressed sister on the cusp of puberty,

bearing the hint of a Lana Turner-like future.
And Mother, vacantly perplexed, stares across

some permanent divide at the one who arrayed them
as if in haste: our aunt's common-law spouse,

I learned five decades later and asked, "Then where
was Dad?" "At home, because he thought I'd been

knocked up"—with the boy she bore in refutation
a full year later. Unseen within the crumpling

of these stories—like a crumb enfolded
in the napkin my mother has propped

before her like a Walküre's shield,
as if to bar all eyes from some unspoken

indignity and for all time deny further witness—
lay her son waiting absently to be born.

August, Late

Already summer's cast
a tattered shroud,
its uncountable green
oblivions against
the patch-quilt sky.

This season's hornet
queen abides inside
the chambered womb
her spittle's made
and anchored with a petiole.

Her court is globed
in chewed-up bark,
fibrous, weathered gray,
like a skull left dangling
by a shank of hair.

How well fear has taught me
not to see something wondrous,
a paper Chinese lantern,
or the floating ark it truly is,
sealed from storm, where cell

by cell, life enjoins itself
to life. My ominous beacon,
immutable moon, I sense
the constant sting of you,
your humming through the air.

Undines

Miscanthus sinensis

Evenings the tasseled grasses concat-
enate light where redwings flared
their shivarees, now flown;
unbraided and brushed by wind,

they caress the afterthought of an
emptiness whose every breath
ignites the air; till the days
darken and the snows break them

I'll watch how they keen the season
the way another once craned when I leant
in close and sent a whisper adrift

along the length of his neck and set
it shuddering—then rode those waves
that swept me drowning in their coils.

ROUTE 1, MILE 0

Rum-punched, I swayed
the length of Duval, amid vacationers
in lazy parade, palm-fronded
in shirts from Fast Buck Freddie's.

What is it about the allure of extremes
that brings me such places: Southernmost
Point, Mile Zero, the sea-snipped end
of a thread fraying into hazy vistas?

In the ambrosial, amnesiac air
of America, don't you love how myth
can mirage such thin horizons? Brighter
than blood, the bougainvilleas spill

around the marker where tourists pose
while pelicans circle overhead like drones,
taking the measure of every errant shimmer.
So many disposable cameras snap and whir.

For now, I am nowhere but here, yet another
place, loaded, awaiting a perfect photo op,
practicing the vacant, inscrutable smile
that might haunt an evening's news.

ARROYO

Some nights I lie in a dry creek bed
at the bottom of a steep ravine
that the passage of my days eroded,

and I imagine the seconds as rain
that long ago thundered away
every last vestige of vegetation,

and yet the dark still teems
with petroglyphs, ochers seared
upon the weathered face of things.

No one sees me here, gray and reptilian
with barely a pulse, nor the stranger
beside me. Such is the vast breadth

of the soul, its inviolable landscape,
till out of some far recess of sleep
a hand strays across my cheek.

TOUCH-ME-NOTS

Impatiens capensis

They begin innocent enough, lowly
splayed leaves, like penitents with palms
upraised, held wide less in pleading
than in the surety grace will fall
from the undercanopy of the trees.

Tenderest catechumens, they absorb all
heaven and earth can afford, brim
like cisterns with spring rain, branch
and rise till each tip bears a jeweled flame.

If you forgive how their zealotry shines
above a strangled light, how the heal-all
and ivies creep withering in their shade,
praise this gardeners' bane—how the blooms
are threaded like lanterns hung for a feast,

tiny cornucopias where hawk moths
and hummingbirds sip through summer
and in the slant-lit hour of dim blue light
pulse like harbingers of frenzied nights,

then fade, swelling day by day to pods—
so seeded and sow-heavy, so tripwire taut,
no devotion you might harbor, no lover's
most loving touch, no secret vow you'd whisper
should forestall the detonations that await you.

Boozed

Six decades, distilled:
joys and sorrows poured

into shapely vessels into which
I peered, through and out toward clear

martini'd worlds where friends
clicked, but then more often down

into smoked peat, the solipsismal
malt in which a single cube of ice

like the soul could melt. How are they
forgotten, all those summer menus,

the savored spice and sweets, trifles
left to nostalgia's oblivion, like lovers,

like the novels I devoured (so many
misremembered plots: her name

and his)? I ate them up and passed
it all like piss and shit, but ah, the delicate

nose of the Pommard that day. Now here,
your eyes. I swear: today I'll quit.

MARLEY'S BEQUESTS

an ampule of my amplest love, a hatbox for your hate,
a cash-box of compassion with hinges rusted shut,
a coffer for your cares, the war-chest of my wiles,
a portmanteau of profit/loss, the diptych of my life,
Canopic jars for jealousies, a locket long unopened
with initials I forget, a closet for your catamite,
a wardrobe for your whores, an iron safe of promises,
its combination lost, a canister of vices, a pillbox
for the poor, this gilded pyx of wafers for communion
with your pride, an iron-lidded casket with who knows
what inside, a ledger for lies, a case of broken vows,
a rucksack for your ridicule, my padlock on remorse,
this crate of insecurities, bankruptcies, misdeeds,
my finest luggage packed with everything you'll need

NEXT HOUSE

The strobe-blue flash
of cruisers, like shrapnel
shot through the house,
became in time a bruise
inflicted faster than panic.

At the church front where
they'd parked, the black
gaps' brief healings fell
between ticks of the clock.
Six dusk-dimmed cops

strode beneath obscene
applause of storm-wet leaves
along a turn in the road, toward
some unknown, something
they learn to look upon

unmoved. And so I let my supper
cool and stood a steady watch
through the nicotined dark,
sure in my knowing
the address and his name.

After the obit came rumors,
like fog with a kelp-laden tang—
how some urologist punctured
his bladder and piss rotted
a nerve. Then pills and depression.

Didn't you see him using a cane?
I saw him hardly at all,
I confessed. And never with crutches,
or the rope, as they claimed,
or the ladder he kicked away.

His Wasted Life

Call it a gesture no one understood,
neither dismissal nor assent, but the thing
left midair when his juggling skewed.

Or call it a broken string of beads,
lost in all directions, his years like coins
clattered on a countertop, misspent.

In hindsight, one might say it haunts
the mists of speculation, a kind of self-
inflicted loathing, or the latticework

he built for a vine to grow, and not
the wind whistling its empty promise
about the life he always wanted.

Storm Fronts

I'd lain in the buff all day, my blanket spread
on wet lawn where the mountainside slopes
to pasture and city boys had come
to camp, escapists all, though most stayed
wired to their wireless ether, channeling
tunes and reports of yet another front approaching.

To the south, I could see a white cloud
spuming up from Vermont Yankee, like a pillar.
Had I been lost in desert, it would've seemed
a providential guide and not the mere exhaust
of an antiquated ideal—like a Polaris
uncocooned from its silo . . . but sun-washed,

I almost found it easy to ignore
what I couldn't tune out: my companions'
iPhoned and -Padded news that dinged from far
beyond the farthest peak, bearing chthonic voices
insistent as the bolts and distant thunder
that were rolling threats across the hollows.

Toward sunset they set out chairs overlooking
the ridged green that ranged for miles
toward nothing they could survive in for long,
stripped as they were, there, of any permanence,
except what they'd been posing for: snap after snap,
their fleeting images jettisoned back into the world.

Almost unnoticed, the phoebes, drab sentinels
of those fields, dotted the fenceposts, ready to snipe
at any insect my passing stirred, while overhead
late squadrons of dragonflies swerved sharp
as lasers upon the humming multitudes.
And so I sat among them, a stranger transfixed

on the day's dazzlements as the sun sifted
unpredictably through banks of Bierstadt hues.
Then night snuck up and closed its jaws around us.
No one saw me slip away or looking back from my tent
toward the banter and play that echoed beneath the bats'
dark and drunken revels above the campfire's glow.

Then came a voice—of a dead man—to shake me:
fear not that lightning cut short your peace,
fear not the rumble of this day's darkness,
from Derry or Damascus, nor the mists that will rise
from the valley at dawn, stained with sadness. Fear
nothing but the cloud-boil that poisons your heart.

WILD CARROT

Daucus carota

See how I abandon
myself, sway so slightly
to some invisible you must surmise,

a melody unvoiced from root
through stalk and stems—what else
should make these umbels teeter

like jellies atop this morning's tide,
lace them with light, that you must posit
tangibles, reasons, the cause? A weed

worth lopping? But spare awhile
the songs you hear moving silent
as shadows beneath me on the ground—

the lore (or lies) about a monarch
pricked by a needle, the tiny bead
of blood transfused and -figured there

upon the whole day's design: a heart
lodged at the core of each florescence.
If not, then brew a teaspoon of my seeds

to abort love's flourishings.
Soon enough this panoply will curl
into dried nests for your dreams.

One gust and every part of me
will detach and tumble in your wake.
You'll find me tenacious. I was meant to be.

Bucolic (with Thistles)

It seemed unnaturally late in October
for such wind-whipped flames: goldfinches
at the roadside, still molten in their breeding
plumage, the males buttery and black
against cloud-swept gray and prickling air.

Where I'd parked to wait out a squall,
I was close enough to see their tongues
at work, assiduously prying at thistles
that spiked the abandoned field. A waste
of effort, I thought, nothing but tares

where wheat had never been, just stabs
of icy rain and those summery hot coals
of yearning for whatever might be teased
from deep within the thorns. But I sat there
even after the idling engine stuttered

me back to awareness the storm had eased.
I'd no schedule to keep, no one waiting.
The road stretched to every place I'd been
hell-bent driving from. And yet, how relentless
desire can be, the need to find in want

some pathway to unwanting, to prize
a stubborn seed of transcendence out
from the fibrous core of one's own being.
In that quiet I could hear the finches, each
chittering an alien gospel of a Kingdom Come—

a dissonance rising on tiny pyroclastic waves
into one atonal choir. A hundred or more
feathered candles flamed atop those spiny heads.
Such raucous burning. What did I sense then
if not the barb of what I thought was happiness?

[30]

MÜNSTERSCHWARZACH

Bavaria

When I need to imagine
heaven, it is always
in reverse: an intaglio
incised on air, its impression
gusting from some otherwhere
bitten in an acid wash
of memory—
            a boy, say,
bent over a bowl of broth,
a face reflected there
freckled with parsley, and all
else in that sacred immensity:
the bare-walled refectory,
the dour Benedictines, a cousin
cowled in graces, *Gott im Himmel*,
words like flesh—
                  smudged away
by time but for that bone-white
plate I drift upon. The illusion
pools at my lips: each vapory
green oasis I sip and savor
though it burns the tongue.

From Wisdom

. . . then he read, *They shall shine and dart*
as sparks through stubble, but I misheard
through stone and thought hard awhile,
thought granite, and tried to let my focus

range beyond the coffin that was lodged
like a slab between us, up toward the stained
glass above the altar, where the sun had spirited
through a single pane, pure as a prism

that shatters light less by volcanic habit
than simple design. So I sat there, amid a field
after gleaning, within a circle of fire I knew
was meant to clear and cleanse and somehow restore

the solid gray of eternity—but for that word, struck
like flint, seeded with *mica, feldspar, quartz.*

Daphnis (with Pan)

National Archaeological Museum, Naples

ἆ δύσερώς τις ἄγαν καὶ ἀμήχανος ἐσσί.
—Theocritus, *Idyll 1*

"Love-sick and adrift" does not begin to capture
how his gaze spills into the hide-strapped reeds
that rise toward his lips, the pitched voids residing there.

Our eyes must puzzle this time-shattered youth back
into place and imagine him quavering in that interval
just before Pan prods his instrument toward the first trill

of a tune. Then we might sense how a god's breath
can hover and his hand compel a comfort that bars escape—
and begin to wonder, Is rapture nothing more than this

enfolding from one emptiness into another? Look.
The boy we reconstruct as yet can barely apprehend
what the god withholds behind a stiff articulation

of hock and hoof, his knee hoisted as if in shame:
how the weight of him verges on immanence,
how creation swells there in want of plundering.

THE SOLITARY

Sainte-Julienne, Québec

At the water's edge a brindled koi loiters
vagrant and alone. All day it's lured me back

to watch it circle the man-made pond
I've camped beside. Its barbels probe

a barren floor. Some thoughtless soul
freed it here, beyond chance of progeny:

black schist blotched with white, yet
in the briefest shudder of its fins, thin

veins of gold dart like flecks in an iris
that rivet attention to the eye's dark core.

The koi wanders within this mirror-world,
a ghost among oak-tops and aspens

that quake upon the surface of the pond
and rewrite what every daub of wind

is busily erasing. —I've drifted for years
through such waters, let illusion settle

like contentment around me while my hand
crimped across the fabric of a page to stitch,

unstitch imperfect threads, the pattern lost
or undetected. Such solitary hungers rimple

just beneath the sheen. Faulty witness, your page
is pure as water; now begin: *A koi caressed the sand.*

RUBY-THROAT

Archilochus colubris

Sudden vibrato
and a start like fear
hot-wiring the spine

thrummed earthward
down to where my fingers
gripped at stubborn roots

among the silent tollings
of the foxgloves' bells
but then those ampules of light

struck through with fiercest
emerald and a flash of red
one by one began to hum

a vespers and the breath
I'd held throttled
just as sudden fled

One Autumn in Ogunquit

the town scrubbed clean
of tourists a tide-washed
stretch of sand the curve

of its blade rubbed smooth
as the glass in my hand
my last ten bucks

for a cocktail some
chitchat and a tune
off-key at a distance

the echo of a room
lust-fueled and lonely
another last sip of gin

neither here nor gone
to heaven his look
when I looked at him

with only the moon
to guide us out
from my lands of the dead

II

Here are your waters and your watering place.
Drink and be whole again beyond confusion.
    —Robert Frost, "Directive"

In Joe's Garden

Unexpected warmth in late November:
a lone cricket basks on an outcrop of granite,
chirring before an audience of two.

Isn't this how we should gladly go,
cricked with an urgent song and soon
silent under our blankets of snow?

So we stoop and groan through this brief
reprieve, hauling tarps of dead uprooted stalks,
the afterfire of goldenrod and black-

eyed Susans, weedy opportunists of neglect
that blurred the shapeliness of once
well-established beds; even the proud

presiding lion with his lichened flanks
had seemed to sink beneath some vast savanna.
But if what we now recultivate indeed

is a form of love, despite the bones' ache,
the sure blights and wilt to come, burrs
that will prick like tiny devils each time

we try to uncover some ideal of what
you first laid out with him so long ago,
know I'm here for you because of him.

Joseph G. Shakra (1934–2004)

DA CAPO

wind riffs through yellow :
    bare limbs bent
to the quick dance of the rain

    bud-break : a tremble
of leaves : the book I left
    at the open window

brailled as if with tears
    : its pages thumbed
by an indifferent hand : this way

    then that under evening
light : should I care my place
    in the story : lost :

like a detail on the river :
    an eddy : its theme
returning on the tide

BUCOLIC (AFTER HEAVY RAIN)

Ah, this lush life
popping like corks
amid the slo-mo
shimmy of slugs
more legato than Satie.

Now chance conspires
incandescences and doom,
shrieks of green and fleeting
respites: yet here we are
again wandering our paths

of ruin, squinting at the sun
among the million zithered
serenades of the season,
cast in its mold, like phlox
scrimmed in untimely snows.

Winds crescendo through
the limbs, and what's past
plinks down like chrism
on upturned heads, on all
that's died and yet would bloom.

Were You a Kind of Galatea

. . . your eyes would be haunted
with an agate haze, landscapes
I could wander, grow lost in
and alarmed I'd perish there
in a flash, in those entanglements
of shade and light we call
the past.
             Your hair'd be patterned loss,
coarse dark I could yet rake
my fingers through and imagine
our couplings reseeded
without end.
                And your skin
would be marble I could pumice
to caressed perfection, the kind
only a span of decades can achieve,
like a veteran who's worried smooth
a scar after many years.
                            If I've forgotten
the precise timbre of that other voice,
how it plucked notes from air,
strung them like garments billowing
on a line, how his penis swelled, its girth
and weight, how I was touched
by slim smiles,
                and if I remember
from time to time how I still love
what is no longer there, it's not because
you are in no way him.

Over Breakfast

... he said, *We need to reinvent
ourselves,* meaning not so much
the *pair* as the *each* of us, as if
we could unroll the raw blue-
print of being, right there
on the table between us
by setting our bowls and cups
at the corners to fix it
in place and staring down
abstract anew the physics of stress
and tolerance into other schemata,
as if time were a constant
and love, an infinite variable
that always yields a positive future,
but one yet together, as if mindfulness
were will and will by necessity
commands action. So we sat, long,
looking each into the other's eyes.

A Shoal

Stenotomus chrysops

At the river's mouth, a shoreward surge
of porgies spilled from the surf

where the tide roiled with bluefish
and harbor seals schooled in ferocities

of hunger. They slashed the quicksilver
flanks of their prey till the air blazed

like shattered mirrors under the angling
sun. We stood on the rocks awhile, safe

in our astonishment, and watched
the sea contuse with the blood of thousands.

Soon there was nothing more to keep us
from the darkened path toward home,

except for the brief flash of the headland within
its gathering sweep, its blind, imperious gaze.

OUROBOROS

Seen from the air, scaled in mercuric glow,
they chasm or snake through untamed
or patterned land, and we can trace both

their birth, writ large and dragonish,
back to snowcaps or shrouded crags
and—looking opposite, to a seeming end,

muddied and diffuse, yet arterial—
their draining into distant horizon
and all boundless beyond;

yet here, banked within a narrow
vision, like the segment of a worm
dissected, is still the paradox

of flux, where each reed bears a vee
in its static wake and stones,
wearied of eternity, ripple

into speech. Sit long enough
and a kingfisher will dive
then shimmer up, fulfilled,

and a whirlwind of midges mating
in a shaft of sunlight will explode
like galaxies in all directions

when a dragonfly darts through their core
and flits off across the water's surface.
Did you notice just now how infinitesimal

death can be? A slash of light in a bird's bill.
A mote gone inside an insect's craw.
And smaller yet, the worry of fry

in their ceaseless scavengings, and the midges,
again summoned back out of chaos,
like electrons circling a necessity.

No Matter How Tight You Shut the Faucet

When a friend asked me to imagine
my very last day, a dream
I try to forget surged from some
backwater synapse of my brain

and though I sat gladly before him—
a deacon at some Church of Christ—
Christ! I thought, picturing me
flat on my intellectual back-

side, drowning in this phlegm
of eschatology. But it was summer
and we were two old friends on the patio
where I'd served us ceviche—

cool, citrusy scallops and shrimp
with diced tomatoes I'd grown
right there beside us, just beyond
the rim of the umbrella's shade—

and I sipped at my sweat-
beaded glass of Tavel as he persisted.
How is it angels can deliver us? *Look*,
I said, pointing over his shoulder. A rose-

breasted grosbeak had appeared
at the feeder. When he turned,
absolved, I noticed the tide
of evening shadows had begun

to rise about our legs, the late
August sun shifting everything

in its thinning light, and I felt alone
even as my friend marveled

at the rarity of the never-seen-before
wonder. The garden spigot I'd failed to fix
drip after drip plashed a mossy bed
of river stones, like intermittent pangs

of guilt recalled. *Richard?* I heard and saw him
stare, unaware I was foundering within another
light, the bead of an idea that had swelled
again at the faucet's lip. How perfect,

I thought, to be held like this, pearled
in tremulous poise, and then suddenly not—
the plummet almost invisible to anyone's eye
till the plosive green reintegration of it all.

BEYOND THAT SLOPE

There's small comfort in the infinite
sameness of change—the river,

down from where our steps lead
through rafts of jewelweed, is passively

indifferent to every sadness we bring
to it; the flat, dull weight of each stone

we toss or skim across its surface
it swallows in the same way a star

ingests a comet: morsel of little moment,
how easily it disappears. Heraclitus

knew but half of it: not how the past swarms,
iridescing, when a man can surrender

to these immersions—how he dissolves
awhile, swept in its flow, glint and swirl—

and emerge to climb the stairs again, rank
with the not-same scent of the same river.

VIRABHADRASANA

To step into this moment,
ease out of time, become

tranced with resolve,
a thought honed to a spear

that every muscle holds
poised, that belies the sinews'

malice, the quenchless feud
flowing between stillness

and intent, and stare dead-on
toward heartless void—even here,

his phalanx arrayed, the warrior
striding on the tide of his breath

may be felled by the merest quiver
sensed quisling through his thigh.

April Aubade

. . . yet again the tiny carillons:
peepers in the predawn
cloister of vernal woods,

their frenzied imperatives
I wake to—a cold-blooded
dissonance of desire

now given full throat
through every synapse
of their being—then sink

on my treading breath
like spawn into the pools
of their mating, silk-spun

trails through night's patch-
work constellations, stars
lost then flashing: cell

upon cell hinging open
onto echoing dark, a nave
I cannot enter, except

like this: brief, uncertain
dawning before the day's first dose
of news, yet here, for now,

beside me,
the sacred hush
of you.

THE ROSE OF SHARON

We argued for weeks, till our differences grew
massive as the shrub itself, a wolf devouring
space and light. Nothing could live beneath
or beside it. Slow to leaf and late to blossom,
prophetess of summer's doom, I loved it nonetheless,
its daily flounce, its brief but lavish blast,
like a dance tune from adolescence, dropping
its cadences everywhere. And I warned, recalling

how my father also claimed an expert knowledge—
that what seems dead, in spring, will rise—and pruned
the old clematis vine, sheared its trellised mat
of midnight sky that cooled our Junes, left
nothing but three gnarled stumps behind.
Now as then, I wait for a sign, some node
nudging through the bark, any least thing
I might love more than the phantomed past.

BELIEFS

Autumn had begun again
glancing blows of sunlight
on the pond we fashioned
broad as a tractor wheel
but shallow, with a bronze
faun to trumpet water
summer-long for three
mottled fish that'd swelled
since May from fingerlings.

We'd watch them breach
the patter, fiery ripples
in play through waning
afternoons into chill October.
Come, we called but they
would not come to feed
after a night scrimmed
our eye into that other-
world with ice.

The nursery's expert
advised we buy a heater
to float and keep a pupil
clear through winter's solid
freezes—a portal for noxious
gas to escape on a wisping
braid of faith—and hope
our Dantean hell retain
a modicum of heaven.

—∭—

Leonardo's Vitruvian Man
could have fit within its circle:
the wicker of a prior winter's
wreath, its plaits storm-brittled,
the willow-bark in frays, rehung
under a side porch and forgotten
till it boiled into song last year
with the *teakettle-teakettle* call
of a wren that had nestled
at the bottom of the giant frame.

That November, the wreath
abandoned, I tossed it
on a burn-pile, but kept
the nest amid the worn-out
gloves and rusty trowels
in my garden bag, propped
in a far corner of the porch.
This spring, hunkered plump
within that nest, amid a puff
of cinnamon, two eyes

stared out at me, unbudgeable
in that instant as my belief
it was the same wren.
All summer she'd come
to the fountain, perch
at the trumpet's brim,
and drink, her tail flicking
like a baton to mark time
for the bright sonata
sluicing from her feet.

—⚭—

Cupped in my hands, a broth
that I whisper upon, its steam
rising like an augury, bearing
the willowy gray-green
up from the bowl's glaze
on which are bossed three
small fish. Caravans once bore
items such as this from China,
celadon so pure it was believed
the vessel would break

if touched by poisoned food.
What manner of death,
I can only imagine, ensued?
And what lesson must I take
along the path today as I plod
near waist-deep in snow
to stare down into that ice-
free ring, so stark and black
against the blinding white
enormity of my disbelief?

Apparition

Lampropeltis triangulum

Such hued cacophony: *coral,*
king, or *milk?* Old mnemonics
fail: "red on black / friend
to Jack, / red on yellow / dangerous
fellow," (but then the mind unspools
"black on red / you'll be dead").

Yet here he lolls in an equinox
of sun and shade, new risen
from a brittle crust of long sleep,
tasting the crisp air, onyx-
eyed, like a starless sky
under which we'd stand immobilized.

Were I to call you, *come and look,*
the shudder passing through
the ground, the shadow of your drawing
near, nothing would remain but a few
words between us, the slough
and void of fearful wonder.

BUCOLIC (WITH MILKWEED)

Unbeautiful, plumped
with toxic alkaloids,

well past empurpling,
these humble wet nurses

serve bristling spawns
of tussock moths. Each

leaf becomes a breast
sucked dry till barely

a rib survives their
tigerish ravening.

What's left are pods,
abandoned rattles,

soundless in September.
Their husks crack and fall

to expose these bursts
of milky floss, spindled

as if on Clotho's wheel
into filaments that bear

the fated seeds
of their renewal.

Year by year the wind-
snagged tether of our gaze

tightens in their wake
even as it frays.

The Augurs

Catkins from birches, pollen from pine
turned the pond to a cauldron brew
that obscured our view of the three
gold fish—those revenant survivors.
How my interest had accrued

like a good investment,
and so I drained the water,
scooped the floundering sinews,
slick in my palms' embrace,
and slid them into a bucket.

I cleaned out muck and reset
stones the weight of winter
had rearranged, filled the black
cavity to its brim, then plugged
the pump back in its socket,

and heard the notes of summer
again spring from the bronze
trumpet of the faun—pellucid
and perfect. I stood and stared
into such sudden clear.

But the fish, within hours, bloated
till their bellies clouded a vast sky.
How did those others sense it,
this feast, those ribbons that unfurled
so quick from chinks in stonework?

I watched them glide upon the water,
watched their jaws unhinge, take hold

and begin the long, relentless swallow.
It was then I heard them mouthing
an absolution I would understand.

A Short Exegesis on the Vanity of the Self

Ever before the world's face,
the self parades its mirror,
would call every thing its own:

that lavender bell, for example,
of the hosta, which just now a bee
approached like a supplicant

with eyes raised toward some
nourishing sublime, the tongue
atremble with evening's flame.

That's how the self crawls inside.
I am not that bee, nor the flower,
nor the silver light that sluiced

through the maple leaves and lit
that flame. Nor the trembling.
And not, any longer, the mirror.

FOUR ASANAS

1. Kakasana

How awkward the body
    bears this solid
graphite sheen, gravid black
    of a crow atop
two spindly branches—like a pinioned
    thought the wind ruffles
till just before unclinching
    it sinks into the pure
weight of stillness, taking flight.

—m—

2. Kapotasana

Always the mimicky stretch
toward otherness, the postured
delve into less creaturely
comfort: this graceless angling
of the leg, the torso's obeisance,
glutes and groin strung
taut as fiddles bowed
into a momentary beauty
wrenched from pain, when breath
surrenders into something like
the cooing of a dove and the mind—
at last, that alien engine—puffs
content within its plaintive song.

—⁓—

3. Halasana

Here the fallow flesh rises
above the mind's dry plottage
to tower briefly, towing heaven
and at zenith arcs earthward
to plant itself sure-footed

there. Now you are passive
soil and solid edge that cleaves
a furrow open to the sky, a bestilled
weight that nonetheless glides, seeding
as it goes the grave of itself.

—∭—

4. Vrksasana

If a mountain can stand
in prayer, what should be
aspired then? Rigidity
begins to sway, and the eye,
yet focused on some distant
anything, triangulates
a balance, attentive
to whatever ambient
currents might move
the limbs; one foot remains
tap-rooted; a thrust knee
burls into absence; and all
the rest branches into
a weightlessness that seems
to dangle from fingertips;
then the mountain stands
like a single hollow reed
siphoning the earth's dark
lightward.

CLAUSTROPHOBIA

The crush of it: not just the body swaddled
in the sweat of fear's embrace, but the thought

confined and bursting within its battered valise,
buckled and strapped for a trip to nowhere

but a smaller place inside a cell where every
pulsing neuron pounds against the tightening vise

of silence—so when you crawled under the house today
to unearth boxes stored with the season's ornaments,

I stood trembling at the sink upstairs, with thoughts
of a past I'd misered away like ingots in a vault.

How can I explain what surges through me,
except to say some memories are airless tombs:

In a dilapidated 70s gray New York Central smoker,
I once sat beside a double-paned window whose seal

had broken. A yard's width of water sloshed to and fro
between those panes, like an aquarium, but compressed.

Upper Manhattan's blind, abandoned tenements lurched
and sped, slowed to a stop, then lurched again, till gone

through dark I arrived at a loveless station. The miracle
of terror is how it feeds on a logic of incongruity:

A mosquito had spawned inside that stagnant space. Just one.
Pale-winged. Tapping the inner surface at the highest edge

of its world. So bloodless, then suddenly inexplicable
and abstract. God, under such weight, my breath shortened—

as here, looking up from the spigot's stream, the colander
brimming with its green absurdities of Brussels sprouts,

I thought I glimpsed again that doomed insect, probing
blankly at your winter-shuttered kitchen window,

and felt once more immured in that bilge-filled railway car
among the bankrupt city's moguls as they ferried between lives

more radiant than I'd ever known. That's how you caught me,
trapped in reflection. That's when you said, *Look what I've found,*

forgotten, and held out some bright, insignificant thing.
—And turning, I opened to you for the first time.

WINTER SOLSTICE

how quick the plummet : moon-sharp
the flint-sparked air : our river crackling
on the full extreme of the tide : how pristine
this burden : snow coiled like a widow's shawl
about the shoulders of the world : how

numbly we face this whiteness : its weather-worn
scars : our fading trajectories : like scavenging
deer : and into it all this rodent-thought
creeps its way out of troubled sleep :
a crosshatch of tunnels : vascular runs

where hunger follows blindly on hunger :
gnaws every tender tendrilling : brutal
and indifferent : like beauty : like this night's
shimmered desolations : like a body : blanketed
yet beneath : so nakedly vulnerable :

how inexorable these silent turnings : as one
from a window : back toward the darkened room :
and returning : the thought : of you : downed in sleep :
as the tide of a sudden snaps the solid mask of things ::
how quick the widdershins flesh tinders into flame.

Adagio in D-major

This is not heaven; we'll hear in it
what we want, what no language
can utter nor searing strings
can tell of pain. Here the wheel
of appearances stops turning
though *langsam* says his score;
so slowly I will enter you, resolved
in the calm of this entwined existence,
in the *ruhevoll* tempo of a distant surf
that rides the onshore winds tonight
farther upriver than we'd have thought.
Thus I've entered, *empfunden*, like a moth
at the window screen, patient but already
consumed in the flame it sought. I'll become
the flow that lifts the curtain, lets it fall,
this music that sweats between us
only to evaporate before it swells again,
rapt, intense, yet seeming to exist
outside of time. And so I'll let it carry us,
till a final beat of the timpani
drums us earthbound back to home.

ACKNOWLEDGMENTS

My thanks to the editors of the following publications in which these poems, some in earlier versions or with different titles, first appeared:

Alabama Literary Review: "Beliefs," "Undines"
American Literary Review: "The Rose of Sharon"
Beloit Poetry Journal: "Winter Solstice"
Blueshift Journal: "Beyond That Slope"
Connotation Press: "Absences," "Apparition," "August, Late," "Marley's Bequests," "Münsterschwarzach," "Next House," "Route I, Mile 0," "A Shoal," "The Solitary," "Touch-me-nots"
CURA: "Four Asanas," "No Matter How Tight You Shut the Faucet," "Summer Solstice"
Green Mountains Review: "Claustrophobia"
The Journal: "His Wasted Life"
The Loft Anthology: New England Poetry and Art: "Male Nude, Kneeling, from the Back"
One: "Bucolic (with Thistles)"
Pea River Journal: "River Road"
Redactions: Poetry & Poetics: "Arroyo," "Boozed"
Redux: A Literary Journal (online reprint): "Winter Solstice"
Shenandoah: "Virabhadrasana"
Southwest Review: "Wild Carrot"
Spillway: "Ruby-throat"
Tar River Poetry: "From Wisdom"
West Branch: "Bucolic (After Heavy Rain)," "Ouroboros," "Over Breakfast," "Storm Fronts"
Whiskey Island Magazine: "Adagio in D-major," "Bucolic (with Milkweed)"

"Male Nude, Kneeling, from the Back" was inspired by a painting of the same title by William Etty, circa 1840 (Yale Center for British Art, New Haven, CT, Bequest of Joseph F. McCrindle).

"Daphnis (with Pan)" was inspired by the copy of Heliodoros's famous sculpture in the National Archaeological Museum of Naples.

"From Wisdom" is for Richard Whitney in memory of his mother.

"Adagio in D-major" incorporates phrases used by Gustav Mahler, Bruno Walter, and John Mangum of the Los Angeles Philharmonic to describe the Third Symphony's last movement.

Special thanks go to Paul Ruffin for his faith in this book, to Sandy Solomon for her insights and advice, to the Virginia Center for the Creative Arts for a residency during which many of these poems were written, and to the National Endowment for the Arts for a fellowship that provided more than financial assistance.

About the Author

Richard Foerster is the author of six previous collections: *Sudden Harbor, Patterns of Descent, Trillium, Double Going, The Burning of Troy,* and *Penetralia* (Texas Review Press, 2011). He has been the recipient of numerous honors, including the "Discovery"/*The Nation* Award, *Poetry* magazine's Bess Hokin Prize, a Maine Arts Commission Fellowship, the Amy Lowell Poetry Travelling Scholarship, and two National Endowment for the Arts poetry fellowships. Since the 1970s his work has appeared widely in magazines and anthologies, including *The Best American Poetry, Kenyon Review, TriQuarterly, The Gettysburg Review, New England Review, The Southern Review,* and *Poetry.* He has worked as a lexicographer, educational writer, typesetter, teacher, and as the editor of the literary magazines *Chelsea* and *Chautauqua Literary Journal.*

—✺—